TEMPLE RUN

DOWNLOADED

EGMONT

We bring stories to life

First published in Great Britain 2014
by Egmont UK Limited
The Yellow Building, One Nicholas Road,
London W1 4AN

ISBN 978 1 4052 4253 0
58315/1
Printed in Italy

WELCOME TO THE TEMPLE

You may feel disorientated having been through the time warp, but do not linger here. Perils beyond your mortal comprehension lurk within these walls and without and many before you have fallen. As you journey through these pages you will find many mental challenges to test your mettle. Quizzes, logic puzzles and code-crackers are all designed to trip you up, but failure is not an option. As you enter the central section you will discover games and stickers to stimulate and entrance, but beware!

Never allow yourself to be turned from your ultimate quest – to discover the golden idols hidden throughout this book. Finding these and deciphering the message they hold will give you a vital clue to surviving in this dangerous dimension.

May the idols bless you with swift feet and unshakeable courage.

Good luck.

WHAT'S IN THIS BOOK?

PUZZLES
From codes and quizzes to mazes and monster wordsearches, this book holds hours of Temple Run puzzling fun.

CREATIVITY
This book offers you many opportunities to get creative. Sketch your own graphic novel, imagine new beasts, then pen new stories about the Temple and its golden idols.

TEMPLE TACTICS

Want to up your gaming prowess? Check out the handy tips and hints that appear throughout the book – they're sure to move you up the Temple Run leaderboard!

PROFILES

Look out for the Runner Fact Files. Each one is packed with everything you need to know about your favourite Temple Run characters.

STICKER ZONE

There are four mega fold-out pages nestled in the middle of the book. Pore over the sheet of peelable Temple Run stickers, then start playing the games and puzzles.

QUEST FOR THE IDOL

There are also 12 golden idols hidden somewhere within these pages. Each is inscribed with a letter. Every time you discover one, turn to page 45 and log the details. By the end of the book, you might just learn their secret.

BRAVE NEW WORLD
WORDSEARCH

Give your grey matter a workout with this mega wordsearch. Twenty Temple Run words, names and phrases are hiding in the grid on the opposite page. Each features in one of the lists below, but you'll have to unscramble the anagrams before you can begin your search! Good luck in your quest.

New to Temple Run? Check out the character profiles.

CHARACTERS

YUG GERSOUNAD

___ _____

CARSTETL OFX

_____ ___

COSFARCIN YATMOON

_____ _____

YRRAB SNOBE

_____ _____

MAARK EEL

_____ ___

HACZ RENDOW

____ _____

LOCATIONS

FATREWLLA

_____

MEIN

____

LETEMP

_____

EDGIRB

_____

YAWWKLA

_____

OBJECTS

NODLEG DOLI

_____ ____

DOUBLER

_____

EMG

___

G E M O T H S U O R E G N A D Y U G
W Z A C H W O N D E R E D L Z N L O
L T D I S L I D E D I R X Z A A K L
X N B P L W O D T E R O O O Y P I D
W O A A I N D N R S F O X O P T N E
J K N M R O I D E T M O T O D Y A N
Y A E I E R E O T B A N O C S I C I
A R S W P A Y E W O O N L E A P A D
E M R S O H L B A M I U O N A R F O
E A R H O R P X O H I N L D I L T L
G L Y T A A N C A N O O S D E S E T
D E E C H Y S T H J E W G T E R M A
I E S H O I N L U E D S H O E R P E
R P E S C A P M D T N K F X O W L N
B E A N O L P A T Y A W K L A W E I
R I A O D G E R F G S P H I L E N M
E R G O W A T E R F A L L S P I R E
F E F T S A F T H T H L S T N U R E

ACTIONS

NUR
_ _ _

PALE
_ _ _ _

MPUJ
_ _ _ _

WIMS
_ _ _ _

DEILS
_ _ _ _ _

TINSRP
_ _ _ _ _ _

TIME WARP

A glitch in time is making it appear that six Temple Runners — Barry Bones, Guy Dangerous, Karma Lee, Scarlett Fox, Francisco Montoya and Montana Smith — are currently together in the same place, but this cannot be. Can you separate each from the others by drawing only three lines across the page?

SURVIVAL QUIZ

Every day in the world of Temple Run is a battle with the unknown. How would you fare if you really found yourself stranded in the wilderness? Test your survival know-how with this quick quiz. Grab a pencil – there's no time to lose!

1 How long can an average person survive without water?

A.   3 days ☐
B.   4 days ☐
C.   5 days ☐

2 Unscramble the words below to reveal the most important survival technique of all.

O D   T N O   C P N I A

_ _   _ _ _   _ _ _ _ _

3 Fire is a vital element in the fight to stay alive in the great outdoors. Besides keeping you warm, name three things it can help you do.

1. ....

2. ....

3. ....

4 Which of these would not be a good source of ready-to-drink water out in the wild?

A.   Rain water ☐
B.   Dew ☐
C.   Water from a stream or river ☐
D.   Snow ☐

5 What helpful element would you discover if you tied a plastic bag over a leafy branch and tied it tightly closed?

....

6 Several small fires provide more heat than one big fire.

A.   True ☐
B.   False ☐

7 If you're lost without a map or compass, what could you use to help you tell which direction was east and which was west?

....

8 Name two things you could use to send an SOS signal.

1. ....

2. ....

POWER PLAY

Only the elite have what it takes to bag precious power play gems as they run! How speedy are your mental maths skills? Give your brainpower a workout with this challenging number box game. Read the rules, grab a pen and get power puzzling!

POWER PLAY RULES

Every vertical and horizontal line of the play board should contain the numbers 1 to 4. The boxed areas containing multiple squares on the board are called 'cages'. The numbers inside each cage must produce the maths rule in the corner. A 5+ in a cage, for example, means that the numbers inside must add up to 5. A 4x means that the numbers in a cage must equal 4 when multiplied together.

4× **1**	5+	2/	
		2−	12×
1−		**1**	**4**
1−		2/ **2**	

TEMPLE TACTICS

About to commence your next run? Need to collect more gems? The Gem Power-up grants gems every time you use it!

LOST LOGIC

Imagine an incredible day where four ultimate runners — Guy Dangerous, Barry Bones, Zach Wonder and Montana Smith — race side-by-side in a bid to escape the Demon Monkey and retain the golden idol for good. Wouldn't it be amazing? This logic puzzle is based on that very notion!

The statements below describe two epic races. Read each one, then see if you can work out the results of each dash.

- Only one runner finished in the same place in both races.

- Guy was never last.

- Barry always beat Zach.

- Montana won Race 1.

- Guy finished third in at least one of the races.

- Both Zach and Barry had a second place.

Write your answers into the leaderboards below.

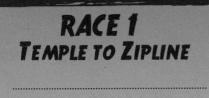

RACE 1
TEMPLE TO ZIPLINE

1 ....

2 ....

3 ....

4 ....

RACE 2
ZIPLINE TO WATERSLIDE

1 ....

2 ....

3 ....

4 ....

MONSTER MAZE

After sprinting his way under crumbling arches, over towering bridges and along creeper-covered walkways, Guy finds himself at the entrance to a stone maze. It seems endless. Can you help him find his way safely to the other side, avoiding the clutches of the demon monkey?

To be transported to the maze opposite, run through the Temple door.

Start

Finish

ICONIC IDOL COLOUR COPY

Once glimpsed, a golden idol should never be forgotten. Commit it to memory by copying the gleaming artefact into the empty grid opposite, square by square.

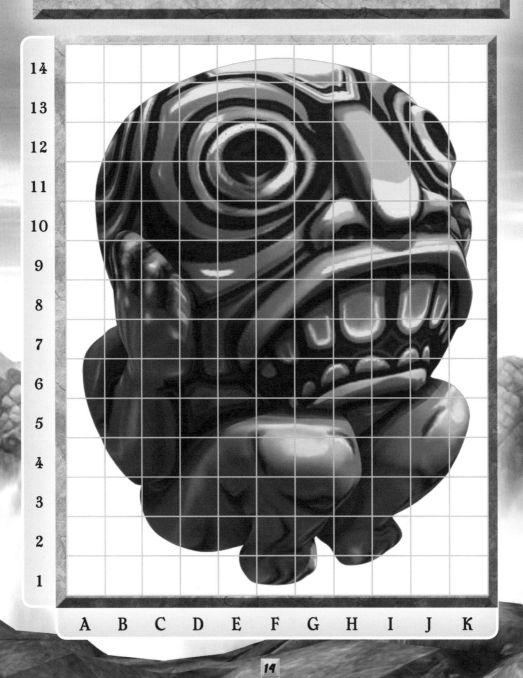

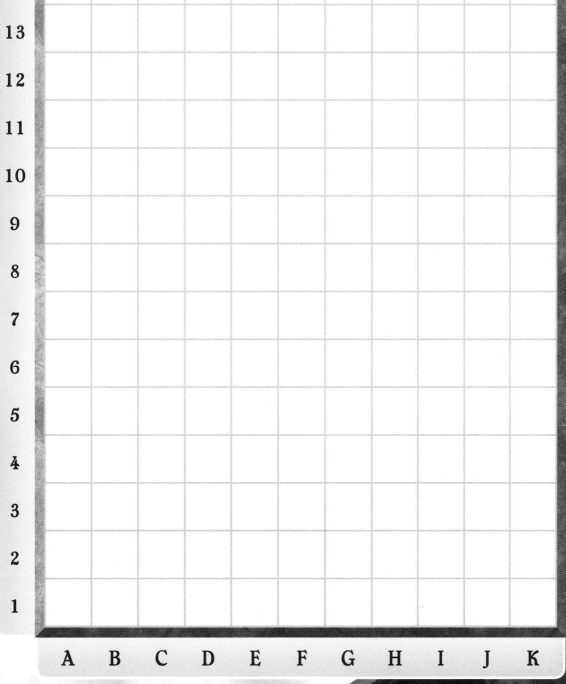

14
13
12
11
10
9
8
7
6
5
4
3
2
1

A B C D E F G H I J K

TEMPLE TILT

You need skill and dexterity to guide a runner through the world of Temple Run. Give your tilting technique a workout with this twisty-turny puzzle page. Can you ace every one?

1. TRICKY SHAPE SHIFTER

How many triangles are contained within the pyramid?

Write your answer here.

3. NUMBER CONUNDRUM

There is only one number between zero and fifty that has all of its letters in alphabetical order. What is it?

2. AMAZING ADDITION

The patterns in the sum below represent a number from 0 to 9. The number is the same wherever the pattern occurs. Can you complete the sum and fill in the missing numbers?

```
_ _ _ _
_ _ _ _  +
```

8 3 ▢ +
2 ▢ ▢
▢ 1 ▢

RUNNER FACT FILE

NAME
Guy Dangerous

SPECIAL SKILLS
Strong will – a born wanderer, Guy's determination helps him survive.

TIME WARPED FROM
2008

COUNTRY OF ORIGIN
Unknown

OTHER INFO
Adventure and peril seem to follow Guy Dangerous wherever he goes - luckily that's just the way he likes it!

4. BIRTHDAY BRAINTEASER

Imagine that the day before yesterday, Scarlett Fox was 27 years old. Next year, she'll turn 30. How can this be possible?

LEAPING LEE

Karma Lee's years of martial arts training have made her super-athletic. Can you work out where each shattered shard of Karma's picture goes? Write the letter of each puzzle piece in the space where it belongs.

A

B

D

C

E

TEMPLE TACTICS
Having trouble with a particular area or level? Remember to leap over flame jets. This will help you through sticky situations – plus you'll look good while you're soaring through the air!

DANGER BEHIND EVERY CORNER

Once again, Guy Dangerous has the mysterious golden idol in his grasp! Clutching it to him he feels a mixture of fear and elation, but then — as he feels sure has happened before — he hears a familiar sound. Something monstrous is on his tail! Guy must run for his life.

GUY KNEW ONE THING... HE HAD TO RUN!

Grab some pens or pencils, then use the panels below to sketch a thrilling chase scene featuring Guy. What form will the demon ape take? How many times will Guy meet his fate at the hands of the monster? Only you can decide.

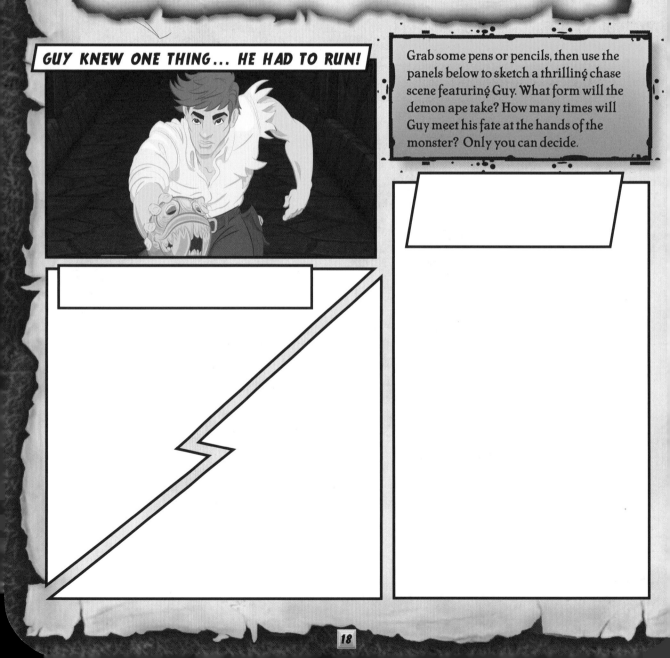

THE CHASE CONTINUED . . .

DESIGN A DEMON

So far, the runners have been pursued by a species of Demon Monkeys, but many other terrifying and fearsome beings could also be lurking in this world. Use this page to imagine and draw a new strange and ferocious creature.

THE LURE OF THE IDOL

Every Temple Runner will tell you that when they encounter a golden idol, they feel a strange force compelling them to snatch it. What magical powers do you think the idols hold? Pick one of the story starters below, then imagine the rest of the legend in your own words.

The first shards of dawn sunlight broke over the Temple, but there was no birdsong today ...

The idol was so far buried in the moss and dirt it was barely visible, yet ...

SCARLETT'S CODE

Scarlett Fox has come up with an amazing new code so that she can leave secret messages for the other runners. Look carefully at the strange symbols below. Can you decipher the message on the opposite page?

INTREPRETING THE CODE

Each letter is represented by the lines around it. The second letter in each space is represented by the lines and a dot. A, for example, looks like a backwards L (⌐). B looks like a backwards L with a dot after it (⌐.).

RUNNER FACT FILE

NAME
Scarlett Fox

SPECIAL SKILLS
Escape Artist – Scarlett uses her sharp wits and cunning to get out of sticky situations.

TIME WARPED FROM
Present day (2008)

COUNTRY OF ORIGIN
Great Britain

OTHER INFO
Scarlett has worked as a corporate spy and a mercenary. She is seductive, intelligent and independent.

AB CD EF
GH IJ KL
MN OP QR

ST
UV WX
YZ

SCARLETT'S MESSAGE

ꓶꓠꓶ ⌄.ꓬꓶ.ꓬ, ꓳ ꓜ.ꓬ⪤ꓡ ꓡ.ꓠ⪤ꓶ.ꓴ ⋀ꓠ⪤ꓦ .ꓬꓡꓛ.ꓠ⪤.ꓡꓴ ꓜ.ꓬ⌄.!

⋀ꓠ⪤ ꓴ.ꓦꓠꓠ.ꓠ.ꓡꓴ ꓳ⌄. ꓳꓶ. ⌄.ꓜ.ꓡ ꓶꓳꓶ.ꓡ.

ꓳ ꓜ.ꓬ⪤ꓡ ꓜ.ꓠꓠꓛꓡꓴ. ꓳ⌄. ꓠꓶ. ꓬ ꓬ.ꓦ.ꓬꓶ.ꓴꓜ.

ꓬ.⋀ ⌄.ꓜ.ꓡ ⪥ꓬ⌄.ꓡꓦ.ꓡ.ꓬꓛꓛ.

_ _ _ _ _ _ _ , _ _ _ _ _ _ _ _ _ _ _ _ _

_ _ _ _ _ _ _ _ _ _ ! _ _ _ _ _ _ _ _ _ _ _ _ _ _

_ _ _ _ _ _ _ . _ _ _ _ _ _ _ _ _ _ _ _ _ _

_ .

Can you pen a reply to Scarlett? Use the code to write one below.

....

....

....

ODD GUY OUT

Guy has entered another dimension and multiplied, but seven of these eight figures have a tiny glitch — only one is the original Guy Dangerous! Use your powers of observation to discover which is the real guy.

A

B

C

D

E

F

G

H

YOUR ANSWER

RUNNER PROFILE

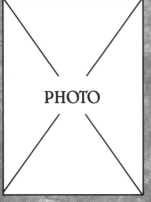

PHOTO

Name: ....

Occupation: ....

A natural born leader with fiery good looks,
I prefer to be active than read stuff in books.
I hail from Great Britain, I'm cunning and sly,
Some say I'm a thief or a corporate spy.

RUNNER PROFILE

Name: ....

Occupation: ....

I'm rough and resourceful, a loner at heart,
I prefer to be outside than in, for a start.
I ride like no other, know cattle as well,
The last guy who crossed me just lay where he fell.

RUNNER PROFILE

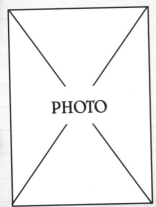

PHOTO

Name: ....

Occupation: ....

Como me llamo? Well come closer do,
Whatever you want to know I will tell you.
But nothing is free in this world or the next,
So pay me in gold coins, 'fore I become vexed.

Temple Runner's Quiz

It's time to test your knowledge about those souls sucked through time to run the gauntlet in this strange land. So far seven intrepid and unique characters are fleeing from the demon monkeys with golden idol in hand. How much do you really know about them? The profiles on the next pages each includes a riddle designed to help you identify the runner. When you've worked out who is being described from the rhyme, update the profile with their name and occupation. Next find their picture from the sticker sheet and put it in place.

Runner Profile

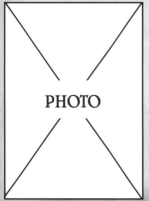

PHOTO

Name: ....

Occupation: ....

I was born and grew up in the US of A, The aim of my game's to make criminals pay. Although I've been three times or more round the block, This realm of the Temple is still a huge shock.

TEMPLE RUN

STICK WITH IT

Daring One,

You have made it to the core. How did you fare? Are you afraid, fatigued, or frustrated? At this point you may well find yourself on the brink of mental exhaustion and you would not be alone. There are many for whom the challenges and perils of this realm are too much. They fall and crumble to dust, are swept away by rising tides or find themselves devoured by creatures of darkness. One way or another, most get consumed by this ancient and mystifying world.

But remember! Nothing is gained by giving up. Take heart, stand fast and turn the page to enter a new fold-out zone of quizzes, puzzles and games. You will need to plunder the sticker sheets in order to succeed. Good luck and may the power of the idols be with you.

Runner Profile

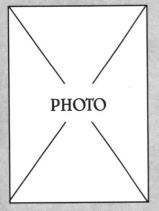

PHOTO

Name: ....

Occupation: ....

Fleeing from monkeys is new I'll admit,
But running's my thing, I'm athletic and fit.
Whether I'm sprinting from monkey or ball,
I know I'll succeed, I'm the strongest of all.

Runner Profile

PHOTO

Name: ....

Occupation: ....

I'm gracious, reserved and it's easy to see,
Why many I meet underestimate me.
For I'm clever, cultured and regal it's true,
But I also know karate and the kung fu.

Runner Profile

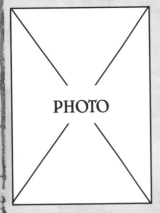

PHOTO

Name: ....

Occupation: ....

I am the original, I was here first,
For thrilling adventure I have a great thirst,
I love to explore, to discover, to roam,
Wherever I lay my hat, that's my home.

Heads Up!

Use this game to really get to grips with Guy Dangerous and his cohorts. Every time you play someone takes on the role of a Temple Run character. The object of the game is to try and work out who the runner is, by asking a series of questions. Sounds easy? Your opponent can only answer with the words 'yes' or 'no'.

Getting Ready to Play
Cut around the dotted lines to create a set of character cards. Have fun decorating them with the stickers in this book.

BARRY
BONES

FRANCISCO
MONTOYA

GUY
DANGEROUS

KARMA
LEE

HOW TO PLAY

1. Shuffle the cards, then place them face down on the table.

2. Take a card each, but do not look at them.

3. Hold your card against your own forehead so the other player can see it.

4. Take it in turns to ask a question to try to guess your identity.

5. Questions must be asked so that the answer is either 'yes' or 'no'. For example, you could ask, 'Do I have brown hair?' but not ... 'What colour is my hair?'

6. The winner is the first to guess their Temple Run identity.

ZACH **WONDER**

SCARLETT **FOX**

MONTANA **SMITH**

THE **PACK**

DEMON **MONKEY**

GOLDEN **IDOL**

	1	2	3	4	5	6	7	8	9	10	11	12	13	14	15
A															
B															
C															
D															
E															
F															
G															
H															
I															
J															
K															
L															
M															
N															
O															

WHAT'S THE BIG IDEA?

Here's your chance to get creative. Can you design your very own Temple Run tee? You'll need a slogan – how about 'DON'T HIDE, RUN!' or 'I RUN THIS TEMPLE'? Add colour and style with stickers and crazy doodles. You could even use this template as a start point for a real customized tee. Awesome!

Golden Grid Game

Brace yourself for the fight of your life! Challenge a friend to a white knuckle co-ordinates game. You'll need to battle to locate your opponent's hidden golden idols before they unearth your own stash. This game requires super strategy and memory skills.

Getting Ready to Play

Find a worthy opponent and grab a pencil each.

Sit opposite each other.

Locate the golden idol stickers and the red circles from the sticker sheet.

Take it in turns to stick your golden idols wherever you like on your 'Player Grid'.

Make sure that the other player does not see where you are sticking them.

How to Play

1 Take it in turns to guess the location of your opponent's idols by stating a grid reference for a square.

2 If the square you have stated does indeed contain part of an idol, the opponent should say 'hit!' and you should mark the square on your 'Opponent's Grid' with an 'X' in pencil. You also take another turn. Meanwhile your opponent should add a red circle sticker on top of the idol on their player grid.

3 If the square you have stated is empty and does not contain part of your opponent's idol, you should mark the square with an 'O' in pencil. Play then passes to your opponent.

4 When a player has found the entire area in which an idol is contained, the opponent must say 'hit and found!'

5 The winner is the first to locate all of their opponent's idols.

Remember! Always give the letter from the horizontal axis first, followed by the number from the vertical axis.

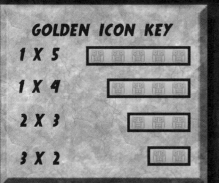

GOLDEN ICON KEY

1 X 5

1 X 4

2 X 3

3 X 2

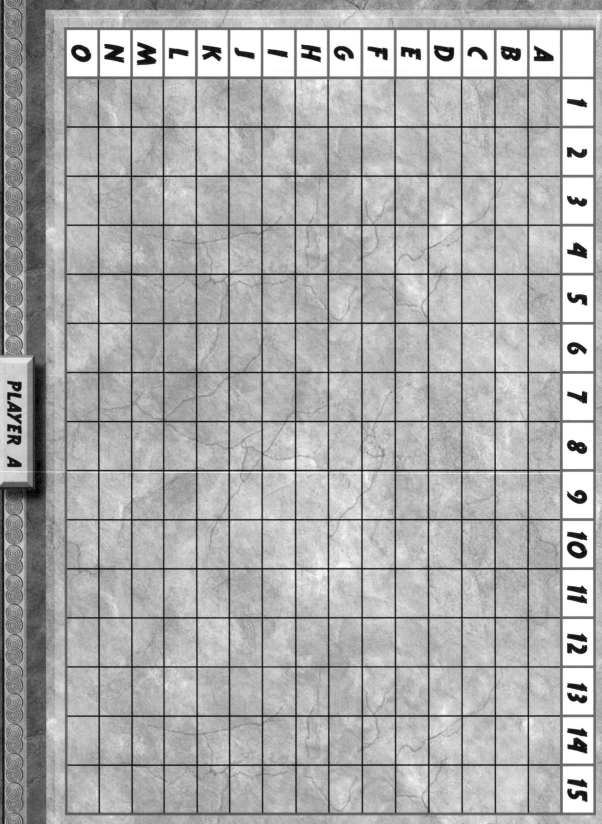

PLAYER A

MEGA STICKER SUDOKU

Can you ace these sticky Sudoku picture puzzles? Use your stickers to complete them. Each mini picture can only appear once in every horizontal and vertical line and in every 3 x 2 mini-grid.

RUNNERS

CREATURES

DANGER

ICONS

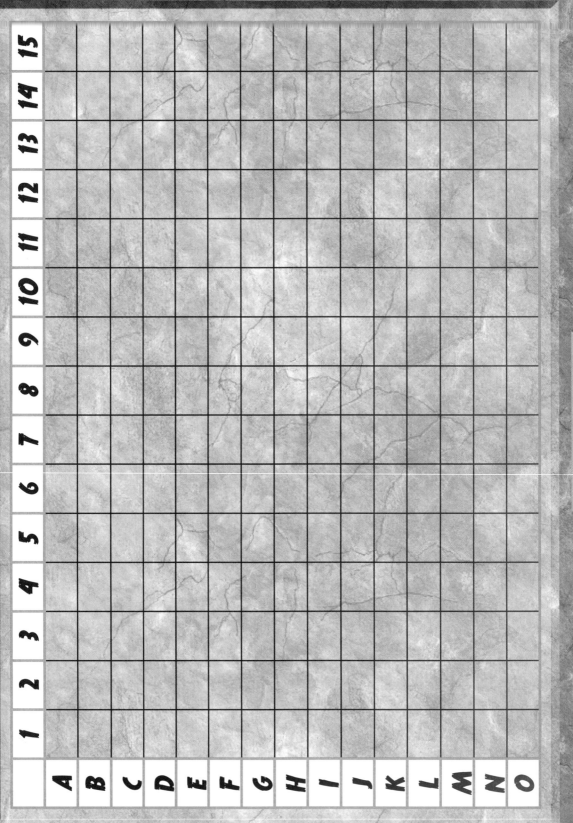

OPPONENT'S GRID

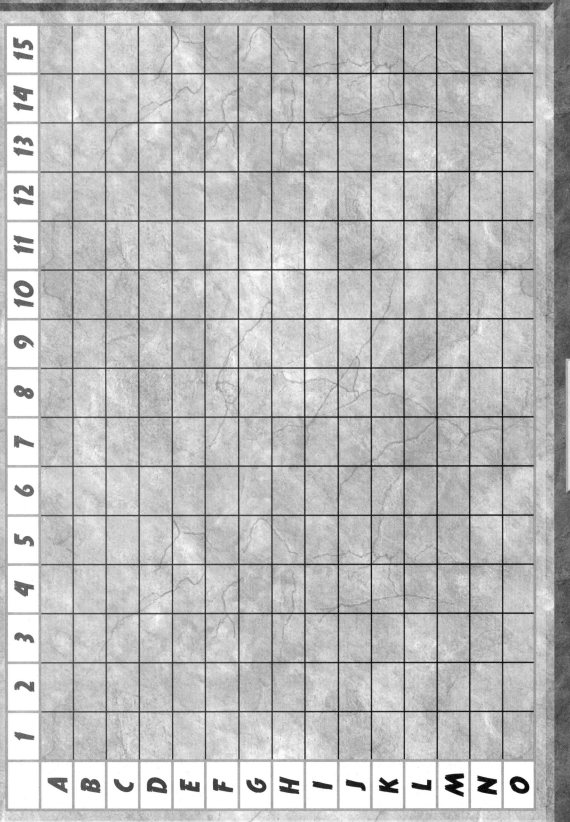

PLAYER B

MONTANA'S MAYHEM

Teetering Temples! Montana's been mobbed by a tribe of demon monkeys. Can you spot the beleaguered explorer before he's reduced to a pile of bones? Once you've found him, deliver the final blow by covering him with one last monkey sticker. Don't worry, he'll regenerate in no time!

BARRY'S BRAINTEASERS

Of all the runners who find themselves at the Mayan Temple, Barry Bones has the most logical mind. Can you ace his top ten brainteasers? If you're struggling to work out an answer, try and think laterally.

You will need a pencil and paper to write the answers down.

1 You walk across a bridge and see a boat full of people, yet there isn't a single person on board. How is that possible?

2 How many golden idols can you fit into an empty box?

3 You are running from the Temple and you overtake Guy Dangerous, who is in second place. What position are you in now?

4 You find yourself trapped on an island in the middle of a huge lake. You cannot swim. One day you escape using nothing but yourself. There is no bridge, boat or raft available to you. How do you do it?

5 A woman is sitting in a house at night. It is pitch black and she has no lamp, light or candle with which to read by. How is she managing to read?

6 Before Mount Everest was discovered, what was the highest mountain in the world?

7 Which questions could never be answered with the word, "yes"?

8 A rooster lays an egg at the top of a mountain. Which slope does it roll down — north, south, east or west?

9 What is the only word in the English language that has six letters — all in alphabetical order?

10 How can FIVE minus TWO equal FOUR?

CART-ASTROPHE

Guy has found himself down a dank and crumbling mine. He needs to navigate the series of underground tunnels in his mine-cart, but the track is incomplete!

Help Guy travel from one end of the mine to the other by laying track either horizontally, vertically or diagonally. Each part of the journey must add up to the number 54. The first section has been completed for you already.

7				3					
	0				7				
		11					18		4
			43	32	1	9			
		11	18						
		35			2	27	14		11
	2	25					50		
START	30	20	4	3	10	47	6		2
	17		49					9	
	9		1					3	R
	21	40	16	17	29	3	8		1
			36		9		9		11

TEMPLE TACTICS

Acing the mine sections of Temple Run is a breeze — as long as you remember to tilt. Instead of holding your device straight as a default position, tilt it to one side while collecting coins or turning. Remain at that angle until you need to tilt to the other side.

2				9		8		
25					13	7		48
39	16					12	1	
		1				5		
		1	41			26		
19	2	52		12		18		
	19			42	7	5		
17	20			10				
	3	14	26	6	8	30	2	7
44	10			13		17		
				17			26	
52				40	10	4	0	3

CONQUISTADOR COINS

Francisco Montoya has an obsessive hunger for gold — you'd better keep your glinting coins out of sight when you play this game! First find a fellow Temple Runner to play with, then collect the coins listed below. Use the opposite page as a score sheet.

YOU WILL NEED

Pencil

1 pence coin

2 pence coin

10 pence coin

20 pence coin

50 pence coin

RUNNER FACT FILE

NAME
Francisco Montoya

SPECIAL SKILLS
Finding gold — Montoya can never get enough to feed his obsession.

TIME WARPED FROM
The past, (early 1500s)

COUNTRY OF ORIGIN
Spain

OTHER INFO
This cruel conquistador is an explorer and adventurer in the service of the Spanish empire. He'll lie, cheat and steal his way to the golden idols.

HOW TO PLAY

1   Take turns to play. The youngest player begins.

2   The first player throws the handful of coins onto the table.

3   Discard all of the coins that land tails up.

4   Points are awarded for any coins that land heads up. If the 2p and 20p land heads up on a turn for example, the score would be 22 points.

5   The winner is the first to reach 500 points.

Player 1

Name: ....

Throw 1	Throw 6 ....
Throw 2	Throw 7 ....
Throw 3	Throw 8 ....
Throw 4	Throw 9 ....
Throw 5	Throw 10 ....

Player 2

Name: ....

Throw 1	Throw 6 ....
Throw 2	Throw 7 ....
Throw 3	Throw 8 ....
Throw 4	Throw 9 ....
Throw 5	Throw 10 ....

A HELPING HAND

Someone has left you a priceless tip in the
Mythical Journal. To gain this valuable knowledge,
you'll need to crack the picture code.

How to puzzle
Identify the character or feature pictured, then write the name
in the space provided. Next add the highlighted letter into the
relevant numbered box. Now you can read the runners' advice.

1. 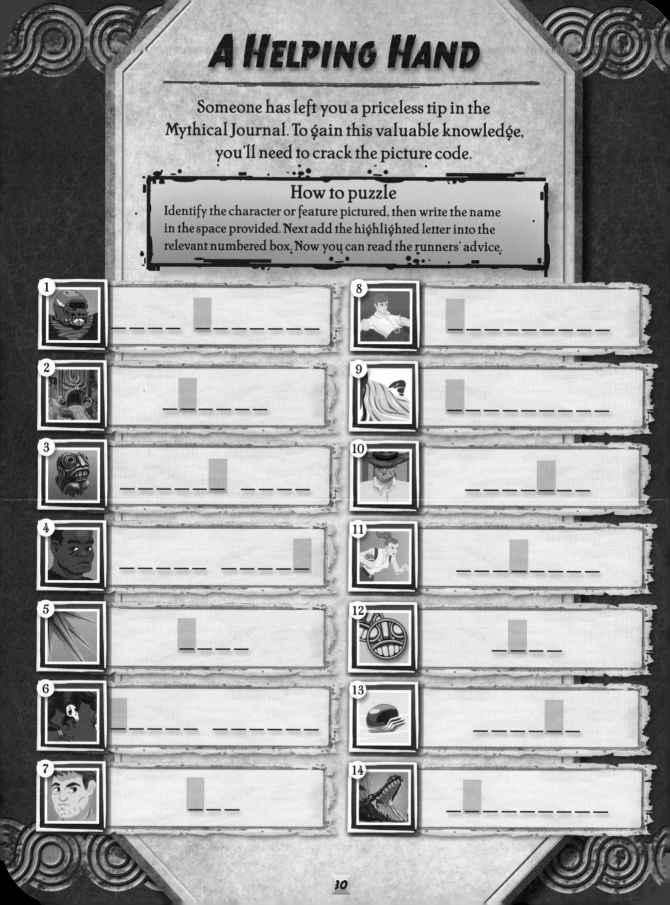 _ _ _ _ _ [_] _ _ _ _ _ _

2. _ _ [_] _ _ _ _

3. _ _ _ _ _ [_] _ _ _

4. _ _ _ _ _ _ _ [_]

5. [_] _ _ _

6. _ _ _ _ _ _

7. [_] _ _

8. _ [_] _ _ _ _ _

9. _ _ _ _ _ _

10. _ _ _ [_] _

11. _ _ [_] _ _ _ _

12. _ _ [_] _ _

13. _ _ _ _ [_] _

14. _ _ _ [_] _ _ _ _

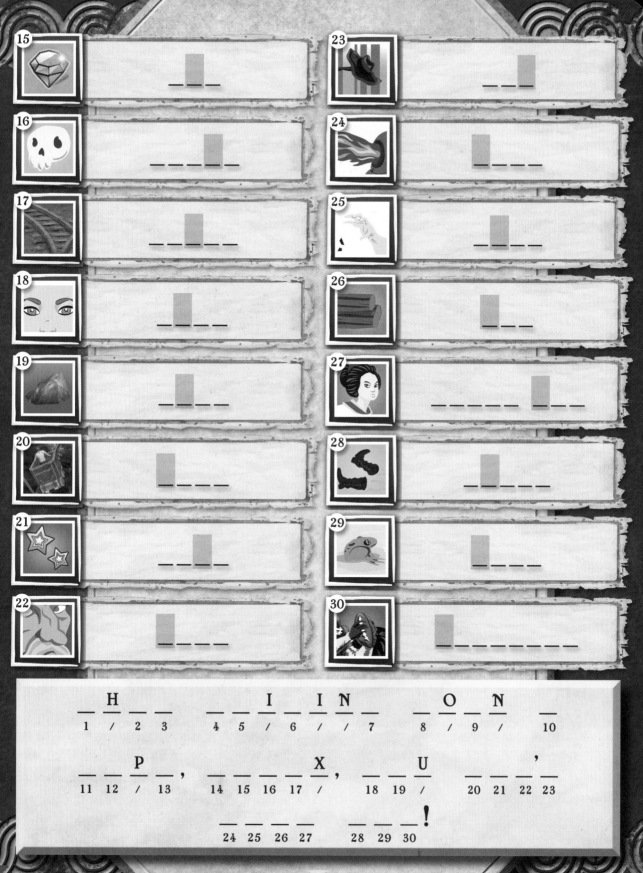

TRICK OF THE LIGHT

Zach Wonder's sporting career has prepared him well for this world. He leaps effortlessly over tree roots and hurls himself fearlessly down ziplines. Can you spot twelve differences between these two images of Zach in action?

RUNNER FACT FILE

NAME
Zach Wonder

SPECIAL SKILLS
Athleticism – an American football star, He combines size, speed and strength to incredible effect.

TIME WARPED FROM
The past (1980s)

COUNTRY OF ORIGIN
United States of America

OTHER INFO
Zach is talented and cool, but he knows it. His cockiness and selfishness may prove his downfall.

A

B

WONDER'S WALL

Zach Wonder's sporting pedigree and innate agility enable him to easily scale any wall or obstacle he meets. Help Zach clamber down the rock face. You'll need to change one letter to form a new word on every step.

The clues next to the wall will guide you on your quest!

HANDS

Nations, countries or territories

Narrow country roads

Decreases gradually in size

Desires

Remains

Lawyers serve these

Clenches teeth

Holding hands tightly

A nagging complaint

To feel about in the dark

A small group of trees

GLOVE

STARTLING SEQUENCE

RUNNER FACT FILE

NAME
Montana Smith

SPECIAL SKILLS
Bushcraft — an outlaw from the Wild West, seasoned Montana knows every survival skill in the book.

TIME WARPED FROM
The past (late 1800s)

COUNTRY OF ORIGIN
United States of America

OTHER INFO
Self-styled as 'the second greatest explorer ever', back home Smith works as a cowboy. He is rough, weathered and bullish.

Even hardened outlaws like Montana Smith admit that the land of Temple Run has a strange and startling beauty. Use your brainpower to transform the nine-letter word at the top of the page into a one-letter word at the bottom. Work your way down slowly, removing one letter at a time to make a new word underneath.

STARTLING

_ _ _ _ _ _ _ _ _

_ _ _ _ _ _ _ _

_ _ _ _ _ _ _

_ _ _ _ _ _

_ _ _ _ _

_ _ _ _

_ _ _

_ _

_

RUN THE RISK

Temple Runners know that if they put a foot wrong, all is lost. You have 60 seconds to answer all of the questions below. If you delay, the monkey is waiting to pounce! Grab a timer or set your mobile, then put your knowledge to the test. How sure-footed are you?

1 The Temple in Temple Run is Gothic.

Yes ☐   No ☐

2 Guy Dangerous is known as the 'second greatest explorer ever'.

Yes ☐   No ☐

3 The large demon monkey from Temple Run 2 is called Cuchanck.

Yes ☐   No ☐

4 Montana Smith comes from Alabama, USA.

Yes ☐   No ☐

5 Besides being caught by monkeys, runners can stumble off the path and meet a sticky end.

Yes ☐   No ☐

6 Zach Wonder is a famous baseball player.

Yes ☐   No ☐

7 Zach Wonder can be cocky and selfish.

Yes ☐   No ☐

8 Karma Lee comes from New China.

Yes ☐   No ☐

9 The characters first learnt that there were others in the same place as them through a mystical journal.

Yes ☐   No ☐

10 Guy Dangerous and Scarlett Fox knew each other before they were time-warped to the Temple.

Yes ☐   No ☐

11 Francisco Montoya is also known as El Dictador.

Yes ☐   No ☐

12 One type of power-up is the Coin Magnet.

Yes ☐   No ☐

13 In her other life, Scarlett Fox works as a waitress.

Yes ☐   No ☐

14 Barry Bones was time-warped from 1980s Miami.

Yes ☐   No ☐

15 In Temple Run 1 the monster chasing the fleeing runners was a wolf.

Yes ☐   No ☐

COMPENDIUM CHALLENGE

Each of the Temple Runners has their own distinct personality. The perplexing puzzles below play to their characteristics. How quickly can you solve them?

1 ZACH'S PHOTO ALBUM

Temple runners don't have time to stop and photograph their surroundings. Can you identify what exactly Zach Wonder has managed to capture on camera?

2 FRANCISCO'S GOLD RUSH

Francisco has a pouch containing ten gold coins. He has ten compatriots who each want a gold coin. He gives each compatriot a gold coin. Afterwards all of his friends have a gold coin each, yet there is still one in the pouch. How?

....

....

....

....

3 KARMA CHAMELEON

Can you spot three differences between these mini pictures of Karma Lee?

TEMPLE TACTICS

· During the water slide, swipe upwards to get your character to re-emerge from the water to begin collecting coins again.

4 MONTANA'S ARROWS

Montana Smith grew up in the Wild West, so he's used to arrows! Follow the pointers to help you unscramble an item often used by cowboys.

A	L	S	B	D	S	G	D	E	A

TEMPLE TACTICS

That pesky monkey keep catching you? Stay one step ahead by combining movements. Did you know that you can turn a corner in the middle of a jump? You can also jump mid-slide if you need to clear an obstacle extra quick!

5 BARRY'S BOXES

Use your visual smarts to detect the common phrases shown here.

MAN
———
BOARD

MEAL

1

PRO M ISE

6 SCARLETT'S SENTENCE

How many words can you make using the letters contained in Scarlett's sentence?

"THIS PLACE IS FRAUGHT WITH DANGER!"

7 GUY'S LETTER GAME

Change one letter in each word to find a totally new term.

LIFT   Change into a present   _ _ _ _

LEAN   Change into a big jump   _ _ _ _

PLAN   Change into a family or group   _ _ _ _

BOLT   Change into a young male horse   _ _ _ _

MAPPING MAYHEM

You have a new mission. Can you complete this crossword? Crack the clues, then use the grid references to position the answers on the map.

The grid reference gives the position of the first letter of the word. The first number in the reference relates to the X co-ordinate and the second number relates to the Y co-ordinate. Some of the words read across and some down. The first one has been done for you.

ACROSS

Francisco MONTOYA is a Spanish Conquistador. (50,100)

The _ _ _ _ _ _ _ _ power-up helps protect you from obstacles. (51,98)

A Temple Runner slides, runs and _ _ _ _ _ _ _ in their quest. (58,98)

The cowboy in Temple Run is called MONTANA _ _ _ _ _ _ _. (60,96)

Runner Scarlett's surname is _ _ _ _ . (62,93)

When a runner is attacked by the demon monkey they might _ _ _ _ _ _ _ _ _ (51,92)

Runners should collect these as they run – _ _ _ _ _ _ _ . (58,91)

Games like Temple Run are known as _ _ _ _ _ _ _ _ _ _ RUNNING GAMES. (53,88)

Mr Dangerous' first name is _ _ _ _ . (55,85)

Ms Fox's colourful first name is _ _ _ _ _ _ _ _ _ _ . (52,83)

DOWN

Various _ _ _ _ _ _ _ _ _ _ _ stand in the runners' way and stop their progress. (51,100)

The ultimate goal of a Temple Run gamer is to be crowned an _ _ _ _ _ _ _ _ _ _ _ _ _ _ _ . (53,98)

In the mines, runners must ride in a _ _ _ _ _ _ .(53,83)

The perilous sounding surname of the default player in Temple Run.

1 and 2 is _ _ _ _ _ _ _ _ _ _ .(55,88)

Another name for a crevasse of the kind runners may fall down – _ _ _ _ _ _ _ .(58,91)

Characters in Temple Run have travelled through _ _ _ _ _ _ to get to the land of the temples. (59,83)

Site of an underground excavation – _ _ _ _ _ _ .(60,92)

Brave and Oz are Temple Run _ _ _ _ _ - _ _ _ _ _ _ .(62,98)

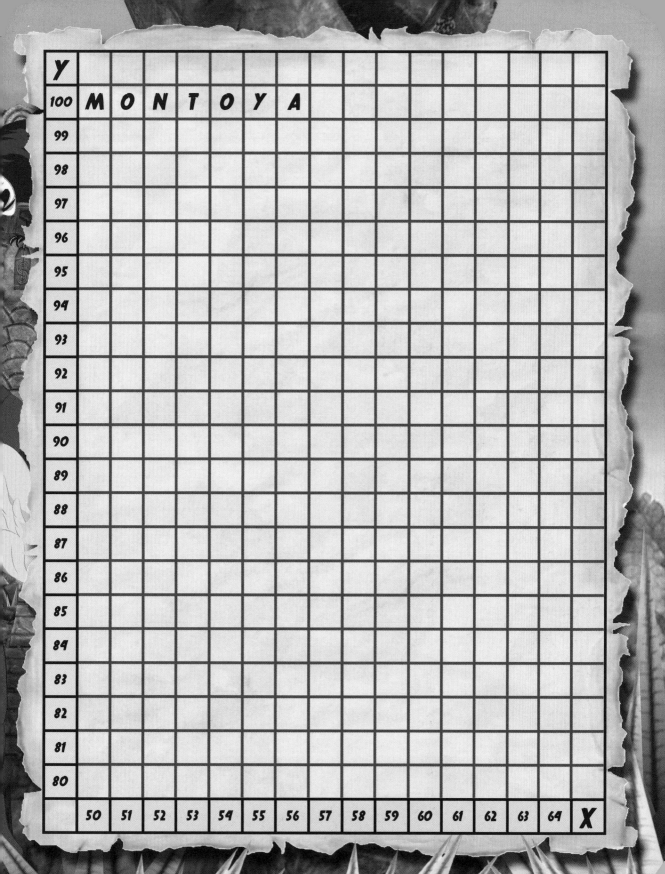

PERILOUS PASTIME

Barry Bones is on the run, but who or what is chasing him? Use these pages to bring to life the perilous scene behind the city cop. Draw in the background and the ferocious foe that's on his tail this time around.

RUNNER FACT FILE

NAME
Barry Bones

SPECIAL SKILLS
Intuition — years working as a detective have made Bones street - smart.

TIME WARPED FROM
1980s

COUNTRY OF ORIGIN
United States of America

OTHER INFO
A city cop with attitude, Bones has seen it all — until now. He's logical, dogged and systematic.

KARMA'S COLOURS

Swift, regal and athletic – not many runners can out-pace Karma Lee! Can you bring the martial arts expert to life? Pick your finest pens and pencils, then use the number key to create a striking colour portrait of the awesome heiress.

RUNNER FACT FILE

NAME
Karma Lee

SPECIAL SKILLS
Speed – she is known as 'the fastest legs in the Far East', Martial Arts Master.

TIME WARPED FROM
The future (2157)

COUNTRY OF ORIGIN
New China

OTHER INFO
Lee is a princess and the heiress of the Great Chameleon Dynasty. She upholds the refined traditions of her people and is a scholar trained in world culture.

1 2 3

4 5

CREEPY CODE

There is only one way to read this code — using an object that has existed for countless ages. Montana Smith must find it in order to read this message, but you will also have one in your home. Can you beat Montana to decipher the code and discover its true provenance?

Temple Runner,

If you are reading this then you are in a strange land dominated by an immense Mayan Temple. Perhaps you already have the golden idol in your grasp and if so, you too will have become 'hunted.' I want to share the knowledge I have gained here. You may not know, but when you reach 2,000 metres you will no longer need to run. You must ride instead. You will find yourself in a cart within a tunnel and so you must tilt artfully to avoid collapsing walls and areas where the metal track has perished. It is both intense and dangerous. I fear there are no limits and no end to this otherworldly adventure — I have undergone countless regenerations already.

Your sister in adventure and peril,

Scarlett Fox

TEMPLE TACTICS

Lean around the red tiles! If you don't react instantly when you see them, it's easy to find yourself floored and then devoured. Jumping over the tiles will work in the early stages of the game, but later on the tiles are often followed by a second object such as a spiked wheel. Leaning around the tiles will help you clear both at the same time.

44

YOUR QUEST

You made it. You may allow yourself to breathe a moment. The idols' awesome power will protect you while you decipher the message inscribed upon them.

Write the inscribed letters in a circle below to help you solve the anagram.

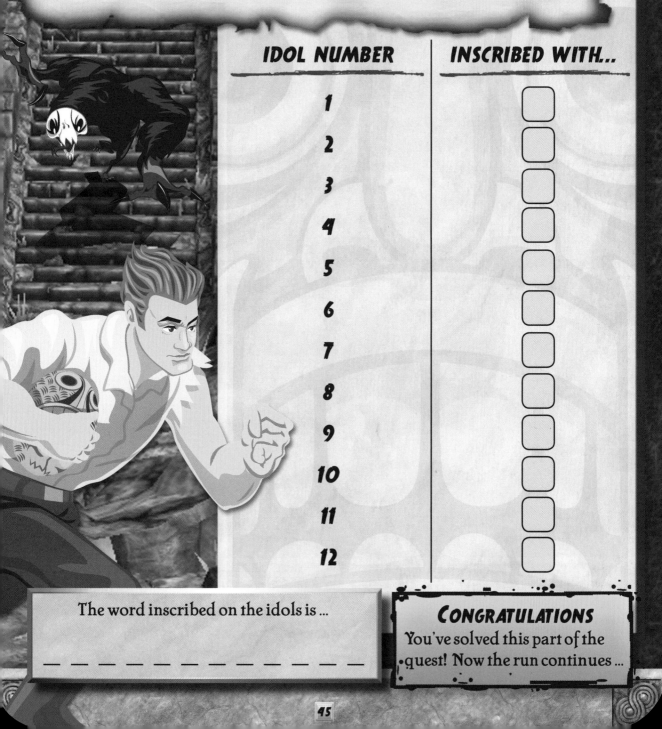

IDOL NUMBER	INSCRIBED WITH...
1	☐
2	☐
3	☐
4	☐
5	☐
6	☐
7	☐
8	☐
9	☐
10	☐
11	☐
12	☐

The word inscribed on the idols is ...

_ _ _ _ _ _ _ _ _ _ _ _

CONGRATULATIONS
You've solved this part of the quest! Now the run continues ...

ANSWERS

Page 6-7
Brave New World Wordsearch

Page 8
Time Warp

Page 9
Survival Quiz
1. A
2. DO NOT PANIC.
   Staying calm will help you think more clearly and stop you making rash decisions.
3. 1. Help see off predators,
   2. Send smoke signals
   3. Boil water
4. C
5. Water. It will have formed as condensation droplets as the plant 'breathes'.
6. True
7. Look at the Sun. It rises in the east and sets in the west, wherever you are on Earth.
8. A mirror reflecting the sun, smoke from a fire, bright items of clothing, sticks and rocks laid out to spell a simple message such as 'HELP'.

Page 10
Power Play

Page 11
Lost Logic
Race 1 – From Temple to Zipline
1. Montana
2. Barry
3. Guy
4. Zach

Race 2 – From Zipline to Waterslide
1. Barry
2. Zach
3. Guy
4. Montana

Explanation:
Since Barry always beat Zach and Zach had a second place, one race must have ended with Barry first and Zach second. Montana therefore won the other race with Barry behind her in second. Since only one runner finished in the same place in both races, this must have been Guy, bagging a third place each time.

Page 12-13
Monster Maze

Page 16
Temple Tilt
1. Tricky Shape Shifter - The pyramid contains 64 triangles.
2. Amazing Addition
   8357
   +792
   9149
3. Number Conundrum - Forty
4. Birthday Brainteaser - Today is January 1st. Yesterday, December 31st, was Scarlett's 28th birthday. That means that this year she'll turn 29 and next year she will be 30.

Page 17
Leaping Lee

Page 22-23
Scarlett's Code
MONTANA, I HAVE FOUND YOUR BELOVED HAT! YOU DROPPED IT IN THE MINE. I HAVE HOOKED IT ON A BRANCH BY THE WATERFALL.

Page 24
Odd Guy Out - E

Gatefold Section
Montana's Mayhem

Mega Sticker Sudoku

7. Guy
8. Dangerous
9. Waterfall
10. Montana
11. Scarlett
12. Coin
13. Helmet
14. Crocodile
15. Gem
16. Skull
17. Track
18. Eyes

19. Rock
20. Cart
21. Stars
22. Nose
23. Hat
24. Fire
25. Hand
26. Log
27. Karma Lee
28. Boots
29. Frog
30. Football

3. →
4. SADDLEBAGS
5. Man overboard
   Square meal
   Hole in one
   Broken promise
6. There are many words that can be formed. Here are a few to get you started:

HEALTH	AUSTRALIAN
CATHEDRAL	TWILIGHT
DRAWING	PRINCESS
CATFISH	CAPITAL

7. LIFT → GIFT
   LEAN → LEAP
   PLAN → CLAN
   BOLT → COLT

Page 38-39
Mapping Mayhem

Page 25
Barry's Brainteasers
1. The people on board are all married.
2. One — after that the box is no longer empty.
3. You are now in second place.
4. You wait for winter. When the lake freezes over, you simply walk away.
5. She is blind and she is using the Braille method.
6. Mount Everest. (It was still there, just not yet discovered.)
7. (a) Are you asleep?
   (b) Are you dead?
8. None. Roosters don't lay eggs!
9. ALMOST
10. Remove F and E and you have IV — roman numerals which mean 4.

Page 32
Trick of the Light

Page 33
Wonder's Wall

HANDS
LANDS
LANES
WANES
WANTS
WAITS
WRITS
GRITS
GRIPS
GRIPE
GROPE
GROVE
GLOVE

Page 34
Startling Sequence

STARTLING
STARTING
STARING
STRING
STING
SING
SIN
IN
I

Page 26-27
Cart-astrophe

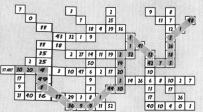

Page 30-31
A Helping Hand
WHEN SLIDING DOWN A ROPE, RELAX, YOU CAN'T FALL OFF!

1. Zach Wonder
2. Temple
3. Golden Idol
4. Barry Bones
5. Leaf
6. Demon Monkey

Page 35
Run the Risk

1. No
2. No
3. Yes
4. No
5. Yes
6. No
7. Yes
8. Yes
9. Yes
10. Yes
11. No
12. Yes
13. No
14. Yes
15. No

Page 36-37
Compendium Challenge
1. It's the demon monkey's tongue.
2. Francisco gave nine of his friends a gold coin. He gave the last one the tenth gold coin in the pouch.

Page 44
Creepy Code
You need a mirror to read the message.

YOUR QUEST ANSWER

P	E	R	S	E	V	E	R	A	N	C	E
1	2	3	4	5	6	7	8	9	10	11	12

The inscribed letters are found on pages 6, 11, 13, 16, 19, 20, 21, 26, 28, 32, 34 and 43.

THE CHASE CONTINUES . . .

FOLLOW THE CONQUEST ON
www.TempleRun.com